Dearest Shaista
haguga
& Kashif

Yummy yumm !!!

Love you all
dearly,

Zeenat
xx

WRITTEN BY
LAURENCE OTTENHEIMER-MAQUET AND RAPHAELLE BRICE,
MARIE FARRE, DOMINIQUE JOLY,
CHRISTINE LAZIER, ODILE LIMOUSIN, GAUD MOREL,
CATHERINE DE SAIRIGNE

ILLUSTRATED BY
DANIELE BOUR, ALAN CRACKNELL, LUC FAUREAU, UTE FUHR AND RAOUL SAUTAI,
DONALD GRANT, PIERRE DE HUGO, AGNES MATHIEU,
RENE METTLER, CLAUDE AND DENISE MILLET, JEAN-PIERRE MOREAU,
SYLVAINE PEROLS, ALINE RIQUIER, JEAN-CLAUDE SENEE,
P. M. VALAT, NATHAELE VOGEL

TRANSLATED AND ADAPTED BY
SARAH GIBSON
WITH SARAH MATTHEWS AND PENNY STANLEY-BAKER

We gratefully acknowledge the advice of:
Dr Andrew Gibson, M.B., B.Chir.
Dr Jane Mainwaring, The Natural History Museum, London
The National Dairy Council
Pauline Sears, Advisory Officer, National Centre for Organic Gardening
Steve Pollock, The Natural History Museum, London
Robert Press, Botanical Consultant
Dr Susanna van Rose, The Geological Museum, London
The Sugar Bureau, London
Geraldine Reid, D.Th.D., Nutritional and Dietary Therapist

ISBN 1 85103 126 X
© 1990 by Editions Gallimard
English text © 1992
by Moonlight Publishing Ltd
First published in Great Britain 1992 by Moonlight Publishing Ltd,
36 Stratford Road, London W8
Cover design by Peter Bennett
Printed in Italy by Editoriale Libraria

OUR FOOD

CONTENTS

MOONLIGHT PUBLISHING

Wheat is the main cereal crop we use to make bread.

Doesn't freshly baked bread smell and taste delicious? People all over the world have eaten bread for centuries. It is one of our basic foods. Bread is made from dough, a mixture of flour and water, which is baked in an oven. Unleavened bread is flat, like a thick pancake. Dough made with yeast* rises, and the loaf is high and rounded. This is the kind we eat most often.

Each type of wheat has a different head of grain; some are bearded, with long, coarse whiskers, some are not.

What is flour made from?

It is made chiefly from grains of wheat. Wheat, like maize, rye and rice, is a type of cereal. Cereal crops are plants which have a head of grain on each stem; the grain can be eaten whole, or ground up to make flour. Each grain of wheat is protected by its husk. Inside the grain is the seed.

A grain of wheat cut in half to show the seed.

How does wheat grow?

The seed begins to develop in the earth, feeding off the grain at first. Gradually it changes into a little green shoot, with roots that draw nourishment from the soil. Finally the tall stems emerge, each topped with a heavy golden ear of grain.

What must the farmer do?

He has to plough the field into long, straight furrows. Then a harrow* breaks up the clods of earth and makes the soil lighter. Now it is ready for seeding. In the old days, farm workers scattered seed by hand. Now farmers use an automatic seed-drill*, which does the job much more quickly.

The furrows are made with a plough.

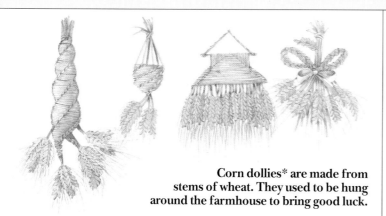

Corn dollies* are made from stems of wheat. They used to be hung around the farmhouse to bring good luck.

Another way to winnow grain is to shake and toss it in a sort of large sieve, called a winnowing-basket. The straw is set aside to feed the animals during the winter.

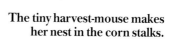

The tiny harvest-mouse makes her nest in the corn stalks.

Now it's time to bring in the harvest!

Even today, wheat is harvested by hand in some countries. It is cut with sickles, and then tied into bundles called sheaves. The whole village helps bring the harvest in, and then it's time to celebrate, with dances, singing and, of course, a special harvest supper!

After the wheat is harvested

Each ear of wheat is made up of forty to sixty grains. Years ago, the sheaves were threshed, or beaten, with long, jointed rods called flails. This freed the grains from the stalks and ears, which were kept as straw.

Then the grain is winnowed.
The next job is to separate the grain from the husks. The workers used to toss the wheat into the air with shovels. The husks are very light so they blew away; the heavier grains fell to the ground.

The wheat is cut with sickles and tied into sheaves.

The sheaves were threshed with flails, and the pile of grain was winnowed.

Today the combine-harvester does the whole job in one day.

A threshing-machine that ran on steam was still a rare sight even 150 years ago, but what a difference it made to the farmers' work! As sheaves were fed into the top, the machine separated the grain from the straw.

The modern combine-harvester does the whole job very quickly. It cuts the corn and collects the grain, leaving the straw behind. The grain is fed into a truck which takes it to the silo to be stored.

At the mill, the wheat grain is ground into flour.

In early times, the grain was crushed between two stones. The Romans invented the millstone: a stone disc which turned on top of another disc to grind the grain. A **water-mill** uses the force of the water current to turn the millstone.

An old-fashioned windmill

If there is no river nearby, the force of the wind can be used to drive the sails of a **windmill.** Both windmills and water-mills have a system of interlocking wheels that make the millstones turn. Modern flour-mills are fully automatic and run on electricity.

The baker prepares the dough with flour and bakes the bread.

The baker works all night long, so that in the morning there's hot, fresh bread ready to sell. He mixes flour with water, salt and yeast* in a machine which kneads it to a firm dough. The dough is shaped into balls, weighed, and left in a warm place for several hours. The yeast gives off tiny bubbles of carbon dioxide gas, which make the dough rise. When the loaves have doubled in size, the baker lifts each one into the oven with a long wooden shovel called a peel.

The baker weighs each piece of dough, and puts it in a warm place where it is left to rise.

The heat of the oven makes the bread crusty. The loaves have to bake for one or two hours, depending on their size. When they come out, the most delicious smell wafts through the bakery!

Inside the bakery

Loaves come in all sorts of different shapes and sizes: tall split loaves, squat cottage loaves, long French sticks. Every country has its own speciality. The sliced bread you buy in supermarkets is usually baked in an industrial bakery.

Look at a slice of bread. Can you see the tiny holes left by the bubbles of gas during baking?

Bread is made from other types of flour too. **Rye** and **oats** are cereal crops which also grow in cold climates. Bread made from rye is dark brown, with a strong, nutty flavour. It is common in Eastern Europe and the Scandinavian countries.

Paddy rice   Brown rice   White rice

What else are cereal crops used for? You need flour to make cakes and pastries. Flour may be refined, white flour, or wholemeal, with the wheat grains and husks still in it. Wholemeal is the best for you. A North  African speciality is **couscous,** made from coarsely ground grains of wheat, which are steamed and served with meat and vegetables. **Millet** grows well in Africa too. It is cooked like a porridge, or baked as unleavened bread.

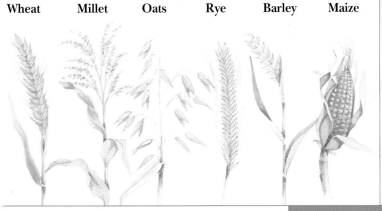

Rice is the most widely grown cereal in Asia. **Maize** is the main cereal used in South America – maize flour is made into flat, thin pancakes called tortillas. You eat them like bread in Mexico. Maize came to Europe in the 16th century, after Christopher Columbus found it growing in America.

Think of all the different kinds of cereal we eat at breakfast! Read the packets to see which grain they are made from: their names may give you a clue!

Once they are dry, maize grains will keep all winter.

Wheat   Millet   Oats   Rye   Barley   Maize

In Asia, people eat rice at every meal.

If you lived in China, India or any other country in Asia, you would eat rice every day: a bowl of simple boiled rice, and sometimes meat, fish or vegetables as well. Rice grows with its roots in the water, in flooded fields called paddy-fields. It is one of the first cereal crops that people ever cultivated*.

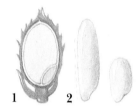

1. A grain of rice cut in half to show its seed.
2. Some types of rice have long grains, other types have round grains.

The kernel of a grain of rice is the part we eat.

Rice plants grow in clumps, each clump producing several ears of grain.
As each grain ripens, it is protected by a fine envelope called a husk.
The grain contains the seed of the new rice plant, and will grow if you plant it.
The stalks of the plant are hollow, so that it can suck up water to feed itself.

The Chinese and Indians have been growing rice for 7,000 years.

The methods of growing rice have not changed much in all that time, and people still enjoy eating it! Merchants, soldiers and sailors brought rice from Asia to the countries they visited. It was first introduced to European countries by the Arabs, about 800 years ago.

In many Asian countries, rice is cooked by steaming it.

Rice is the staple food for more than half the world's people.

Rice is grown
in countries with
warm climates.

Today, nine out of every ten sacks of rice are grown in Asia.
The Asians eat almost all the rice they grow.

A huge amount of rice is grown in the United States, too, but a lot of it is sold to the rest of the world.

Herons, wild duck, frogs and fish all make their homes in the paddy-fields... and so do thousands of mosquitoes!

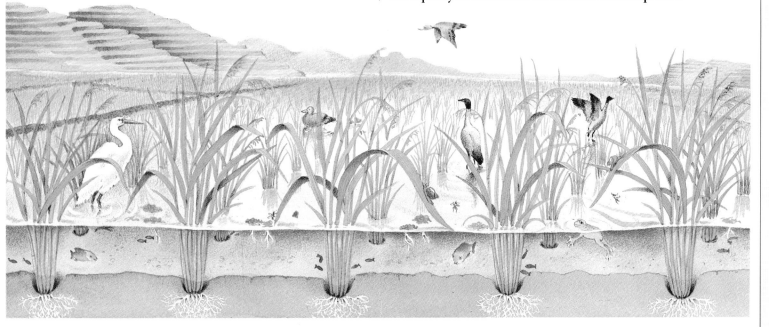

Many hands are needed to look after the paddy-fields...

First, the paddy-field is flooded.

Ditches carry the water from the rivers to the fields. The low barriers across these ditches can be raised to let the water flow into the fields.

After the fields have been flooded, the workers plough, rake and flatten the muddy soil, with the help of ploughs, harrows* and rollers pulled by buffaloes. While the paddy-fields are being prepared, the rice is sown in a separate flooded field called the seed-bed.

The seedlings have to be planted out.

After a month, the young rice plants have grown, but they are too close together and need more room to develop properly. They have to be lifted and transplanted to the paddy-field. It's back-breaking work! Bent double, ankle-deep in water, women plant out the seedlings in straight lines, leaving them plenty of space to grow.

The water helps to keep down the weeds.

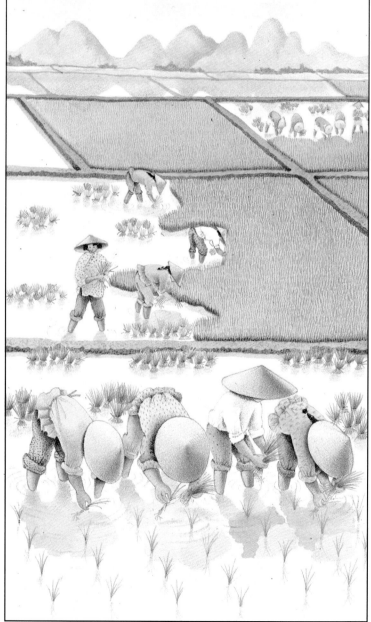

The harvest

Three to six months later, the rice has turned golden and the heads are heavy with grain. The rice is ripe for harvesting. Just before the harvest, sluice gates in the ditches are opened, and the water drains out of the paddy-fields back into the river. The mud dries and hardens. From dawn till dusk, the rice-growers cut the stalks with sickles and tie the plants into bundles. The crop is carried back to the village.

The cut rice stalks are beaten against a stone roller to shake off all the grain. They are stacked and kept for straw, while the grain is left out in the sun to dry. Later, the loose grain is crushed in a mortar with a pestle to free the kernels from the husks. Then it is winnowed. At this stage, it is brown, whole-grain rice. To make white rice, the last fine pieces of husk have to be removed.

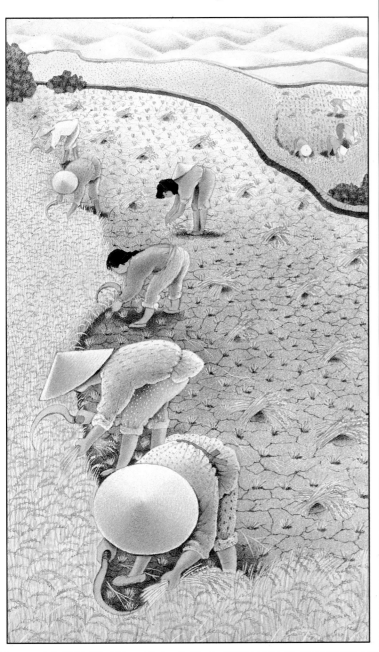

In Asia, rice is even grown high up in the mountains.

People in Asia use rice in all sorts of different ways.

Damaged grains of rice are fermented* for beer, or ground into flour to make cakes and noodles. Rice-straw is woven into baskets and hats. Rice husks are used to feed animals, or to make fertilizer*. Rice is so important in some countries that farmers build terraces on hills and mountains so that even there rice can be grown in paddy-fields. Spring water runs down the terraces in channels.

In the United States of America, rice is grown in huge fields.

Nearly everything is done with enormous machines. The rice fields are raked and harrowed* by tractors.

Whether they are up a mountainside or on the plain, paddy-fields have to be level.

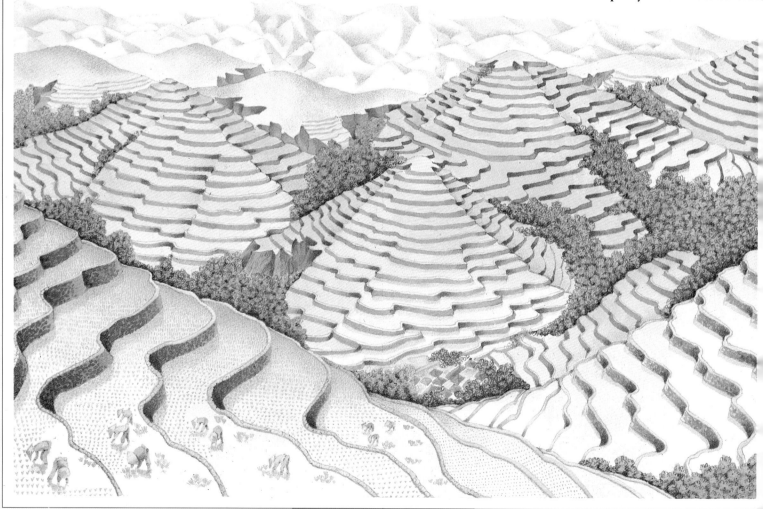

16

A machine digs channels in the fields. Then water floods through them from a big pipe.

The rice germinates* in sacks soaking in water.

Aeroplanes fly low over the fields to sow the rice. This method cuts out the need to replant by hand, which involves a lot of costly labour.

Combine-harvesters gather the ripe plants and automatically separate the straw from the grain. In the factory, the rice is dried, husked and put into packets.

Rice festivals

In Asia, rice is such an important crop that people organize festivals to ask the gods for a good harvest. Rice may be stored in special granaries which are built on stilts to protect their precious contents from floods and hungry animals.

In Europe and America, rice is thrown over newly married couples to bring them good luck.

A granary on the island of Sulawesi, Indonesia

Potatoes grow under the ground.

The word potato is one we have borrowed from the South American Indians who first grew and used the plant.
You can't eat raw potatoes, but there are lots of different ways of cooking them. Do you like chips, fried in oil until they are crispy? Or a potato baked in the oven in its skin?

A potato is a tuber. It is part of the plant's underground stem which has swollen. Potato plants do have a fruit, which looks like a small green tomato. Watch out though! Potato fruit is poisonous.

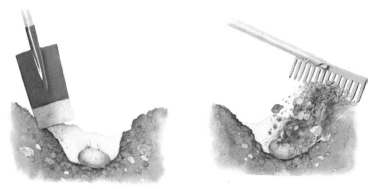

If you plant a potato in the soil, you will end up with fifteen to twenty new ones.
A shoot pushes up through the soil, growing into a stem.

One of last year's potatoes is planted in spring. Soon, a shoot appears.

The shoot feeds on the goodness stored in the old potato, which gradually shrivels up as the plant develops.
The roots grow and begin to swell into tiny new potatoes. It is a good idea to heap a small mound of earth around the base of the plant, because if light gets to the young potatoes they will turn green, and will not be good to eat.

In autumn, the plant turns yellow and its leaves wither. This is the signal that the potatoes are fully grown, with strong skins. Now it's time to dig them up.

In the old days, potatoes were harvested by hand.

Harvesting potatoes

Before farm machines were invented, people had to dig up, or lift, potatoes with a fork. They were left out to dry in the fields before being sorted. Some were kept as seed potatoes for next year's crop. Any that were damaged were fed to the animals, and the rest were kept for eating. For a long while, though, potatoes were thought to be a food that only poor people ate. It's only in the last hundred years that they have become really popular.

Have you noticed that there are many different varieties of potato for sale in the shops?

New potatoes are picked before they are full-grown. Their skins are thin and are hardly a protection for them. They taste delicious, but don't keep for long. Other potatoes store well for up to a year in a dry and dark place, like a cellar. Some types of potato are firm and make good chips or roast potatoes. Others break down as they cook and are better mashed, baked, or used in soup.

The potato comes from South America.
Long ago, the Inca* people of Peru, in South America, found they were able to grow small potatoes high up in the mountains, to feed themselves and their animals.

The Spanish discovered the potato when they went to South America.
In the middle of the 16th century, General Pizarro and his soldiers set out from Spain to conquer the newly discovered lands of South America. They found the Incas growing a vegetable they called 'batata': the potato.
By about 1570, potatoes and other wonders from the New World were arriving by ship in Europe.

The Indians in Peru today, many of them descendants of the Incas, dry their potatoes so that they keep for years. They tread them to press out the water, then they leave them out over several nights to freeze.

This strange foreign vegetable was not popular in Europe at first.
For a long time, the peasants thought this new vegetable would make them ill. They fed potatoes to their pigs rather than eating them themselves, even during years of famine!
Then, in the 17th century, a French scientist called André Parmentier had an idea. He set guards round the potato fields, pretending there was something precious growing. Eager to find out what was so special, the peasants crept in at night and stole some potatoes.
They soon found out that they were good to eat after all!

On a modern farm, special machines harvest the potatoes.

They separate the potatoes from stones and lumps of earth. In the factory, a sorting machine grades the potatoes according to their size. Any that are green or an odd shape are taken out by hand and are not sent for sale. Some potatoes are set aside to make potato powder. First they are boiled, then mashed and finally dried out in a hot-air machine.

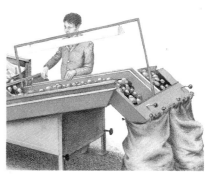

Colorado beetle eggs

Larva

The Colorado beetle: the potato's worst enemy.

Thirty beetle larvae can devour a whole potato plant in a week.
The female beetle lays 2,500 eggs. In six weeks, 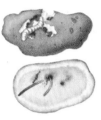 they have hatched into larvae, which then grow into beetles and lay eggs in their turn. Worms and slugs eat potatoes too. Today, we spray crops with chemicals to kill pests and control diseases like potato blight.

Luckily wasps, gadflies and ladybirds like to eat the larvae of Colorado beetles.

Look at the different shapes and colours potatoes can be!

There are many different varieties of potato. All contain vitamins*, and fibre* and the carbohydrate*, starch. Purified starch is a white powder. As it is smooth, absorbent and gluey, it can be used for all sorts of things; there is starch in sauces, soups, cakes and ice-cream, as well as in glue, cardboard and even disposable nappies! **Scientists are working to create new varieties of potato which will be better able to resist disease.** They take the pollen* from one

potato flower and place it carefully on the flower of another variety. This is called cross-fertilization. The new seeds collected from the fruit are kept in test-tubes where they develop into seedlings. These are moved to greenhouses until they are strong enough to grow outside.

Growing potatoes in a test-tube.

Sometimes scientists lift a shoot from a full-grown potato and place it in a test-tube on special jelly. Three weeks later, new shoots have sprouted. These are planted out in pots. When the leaves and roots appear, they are divided into new plants. In this way, two million plants can be grown from a single shoot in less than a year.

Potatoes store well in a cool, dark place.

Flowers fade and grow into fruits...

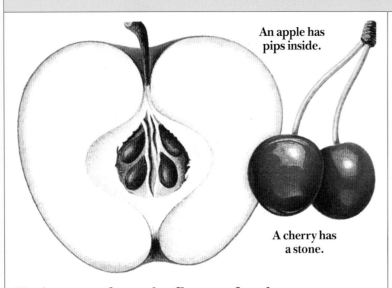

An apple has pips inside.

A cherry has a stone.

Fruit comes from the flower of a plant.

Many kinds of plants grow flowers, which turn into fruit with seeds inside. The seeds will grow into new plants if they germinate*. The fruit protects and feeds the seed as it develops. The seeds of some fruits, like grapes, currants or melons, are what we call the pips. The seed of a cherry or a plum grows inside a hard shell, which we call the stone. Raspberries and blackberries are made up of a mass of little fruits all joined together, each with its own pip.

Quince

Apricot

Greengage

Peach

Pear

Mirabelle plum

Plum

Redcurrants

Gooseberries

Blackcurrants

Strawberries

Raspberries

Fresh fruit contains a lot of vitamins* that are important for our health.

Lemons in particular are bursting with Vitamin C. In the past, sailors took them on long sea voyages, because without Vitamin C they risked developing a disease called scurvy. A Kiwi fruit has twice as much Vitamin C as an orange.

We eat fruit when it is ripe.

That is when it is soft and sweet. Some fruits are picked before they have ripened naturally on the tree; bananas are picked while they are green, and finish ripening on their long journey to market. Fruit like mangoes or lychees, which come from hot countries, travel in chilled containers; this helps keep the fruit fresh, and kills any insects which might harm them.

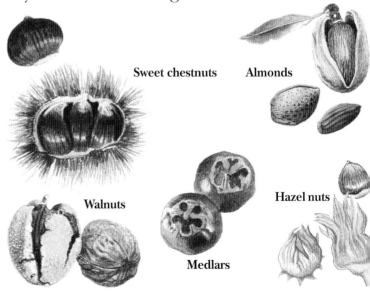

Sweet chestnuts

Almonds

Walnuts

Medlars

Hazel nuts

Apples and pears are stored at a low temperature for the same reason. In this way, the fruit can be kept in a good state for several months after it has been picked.

Once it is ripe, fruit must be quickly eaten or stored. Heating it is a way of preserving it. If fruit is cooked, the heat sterilizes it, killing the bacteria which make it go bad. Sugar will help it keep too. That is why jam and bottled fruit can be kept so long. Heat-treated fruit is also used in ice-creams and yoghurts. Fruit can be squeezed and crushed to make fruit juice drinks.

Grape juice can be made into wine. Grapes are picked in the autumn, when they are ripe and full of sugary juice. After they are crushed, the juice begins to ferment* and turns into alcohol. It is put in barrels, then bottled, to allow it to age and mature. Apple juice can be made into cider.

Grapes

Watermelon

Melon

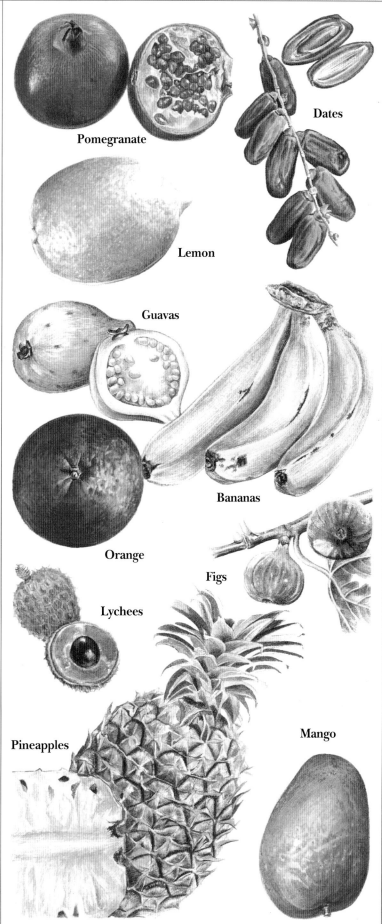

Pomegranate

Dates

Lemon

Guavas

Bananas

Orange

Figs

Lychees

Pineapples

Mango

25

Vegetables were cultivated from wild plants long ago.

Vegetables are part of our daily diet, whether we eat them raw or cooked, fresh, frozen or from a tin. They are vital for our health, because of the many vitamins* and minerals* they contain.

They originated from wild plants: sea-cabbage growing on the sand-dunes, for instance, gave us cauliflower and broccoli. Over centuries, people picked out the wild plants that were best to eat. They collected seeds from the strongest plants, sowed them, and slowly new varieties evolved.

Artichoke
Tomato
Chilli pepper
Aubergine
Courgette

Which part of a vegetable do we eat? That depends on the vegetable. We eat the leaves of cabbages, spinach and leeks. We eat the root of carrots, beetroot and radishes, but the fruit of tomatoes, aubergines, cucumbers and courgettes. Have you noticed seeds in them? An onion, or a clove of garlic, is the bulb of the plant, and an artichoke is actually a flower! Peas are seeds, beans are seed pods, Brussels sprouts, with their small, tightly packed leaves, are buds.

Lentils
Mange-tout
Peas
Broad beans
Haricot beans

Do you know what a kitchen garden is? It is a part of the garden kept especially for growing fruit and vegetables, often with a wall around it.

Nowadays, most of the fresh vegetables we eat have been grown on a large scale in fields, harvested by machines, sold at market and sent to the shops. But some people still prefer to grow their own fresh produce in their allotment or garden.

Today some are grown under glass, some in the open fields.

We like to be able to eat salad vegetables all year round.

They have to be grown in greenhouses or in fields under tunnels of plastic which hold the sun's warmth. Asparagus shoots start to stir in the spring. Some are kept covered with soil, and because they have had no light, they grow into long, white stems, tender to eat. Button mushrooms are also grown in the dark, in cellars, to stop them opening out.

Most vegetables contain fibre*.

Fibre is vital if our digestive system is to work well. It helps food to pass through the gut quickly and efficiently.
Lentils, broad beans, kidney beans, cabbage and spinach are all particularly high in fibre.

Endive

Cauliflower

Cabbage

Brussels sprouts

Lamb's lettuce

Lettuce

Sorrel

Spinach

Leek

Garlic

Shallot

Onion

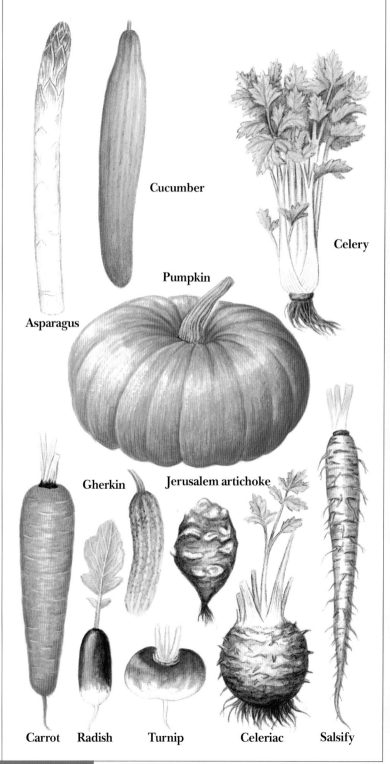

Asparagus

Cucumber

Celery

Pumpkin

Gherkin

Jerusalem artichoke

Carrot

Radish

Turnip

Celeriac

Salsify

27

A gardener's tasks vary as the year goes round.

Spring is the busiest time of the year! A gardener has to sow the seeds which will grow into peas (1), beans (3) and carrots (6), and plant out potatoes (2) and onions (7). Radishes (8) and lettuces (5) still need to be shielded from the cold by glass frames or plastic sheeting until the weather is warmer. Strawberries (4) and other fruits can be netted to protect them from birds, who love to feast on the ripe berries.

The warmth of the summer sun helps everything grow in the garden. Plants flourish in the sunshine, but so do the weeds! They have to be pulled out. Strawberries ripen. Beans and lettuces are ready for picking. Onions, carrots and radishes are ready now, too. The potato plants are in flower. In dry spells, the beds should be watered every evening, when the sun is not so hot; plants hate the soil to be too dry and hard.

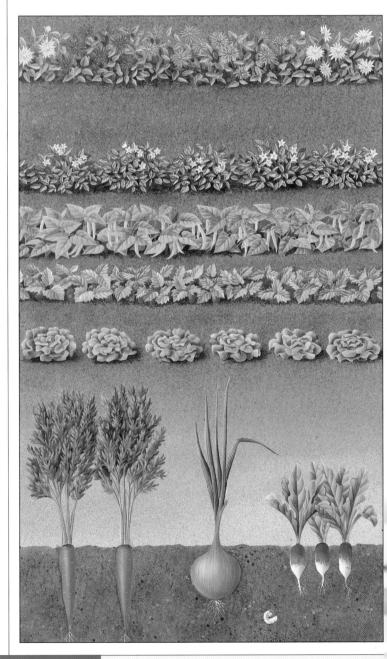

Each fruit and vegetable has its season.

In autumn, the days grow shorter.

The nights are getting colder. It's time to plant cabbages (1), leeks (2) and winter salad (3). The gardener digs manure or garden compost into the soil, to put back some of the nourishment the plants have used during the year.

In a corner of the kitchen garden, there might be room for some flowers, like dahlias and chrysanthemums, to give a last burst of colour before winter sets in.

Dibber for making holes in the soil

In winter, the earth is at rest.

Cold numbs the plants, trees lose their leaves, and nature seems to have fallen asleep. Only birds and small animals show signs of life. The gardener digs over the ground to prepare it for planting in the spring. He cuts off the chicory leaves, and plants the roots in a dark box. The new leaves that shoot up stay white, because they have had no light. This is the vegetable we call endive. It's delicious in a winter salad.

Garden spade

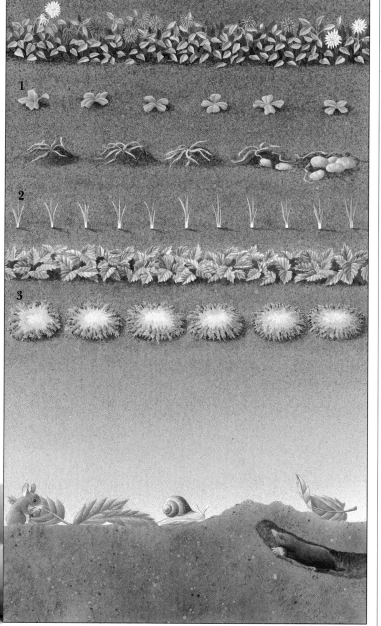

Ever since prehistoric times, people have used animals for food. They believed that some of the animal's strength would pass on to them if they ate its meat.

This cave painting in the Lascaux cave, in France, is at least 15,00 years old.

Paintings on the walls of prehistoric caves are often of wild animals like bison, stags and boars. Most of the people who lived in these caves were hunters. They used almost every part of the animals they killed: the meat, fat, bone and horn, skin and fur. But they did not know how to stop food going bad, and they risked starvation if the hunting was poor. Gradually they learned to keep flocks of animals – pigs, sheep, goats and cattle, and to domesticate* them.

Prehistoric people painted animals on the walls of their caves to bring them luck when they went hunting.

People began to rear animals, and their way of life changed.

They spent more time looking after their herds and growing crops, instead of gathering wild plants for food. Once they had been nomads, wandering the land. Now they settled in one place and villages began to spring up. With their stores of grain and a supply of meat and milk from their flocks, people were less and less dependent on hunting and gathering food from the wild. They started to cut down trees to make larger fields and pastures for their herds of animals.

Here are some examples of the different types of meat that come from beef:

Sirloin   Chuck steak   Steak   Hamburger

Rib roast   Fillet   Rib   Veal (calf)

People have been raising domestic animals for about 6,000 years.

Skilful rearing and crossing of breeds has meant that the animals have changed. The aurochs, the wild ancestor of our domestic cow, is now extinct. There are many new breeds, some reared especially for their succulent meat. Beef is rich in iron, an important mineral* in our diet, which helps us produce red blood cells.

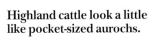
Highland cattle look a little like pocket-sized aurochs.

Simmental (beef and milk)   German Yellow (beef)

West Highland (mainly beef)   Aberdeen Angus (beef)

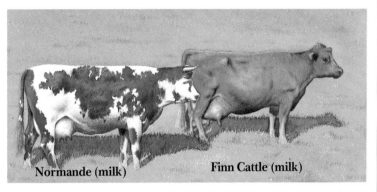
Normande (milk)   Finn Cattle (milk)

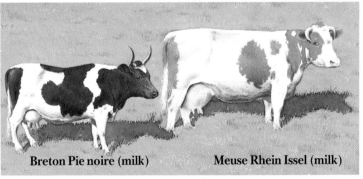
Breton Pie noire (milk)   Meuse Rhein Issel (milk)

Charolais (beef)   Hereford (beef)

Pigs were the first animals to be reared by man.

One in three of all the pigs in the world lives in China. They have been reared there for thousands of years. Pigs have been raised for meat in Europe for a long time too. In the Middle Ages, they roamed the forests in the care of a swineherd, or wandered about the streets of the towns. They looked rather like their ancestor, the wild boar. Nowadays, most pigs live in sties on farms.

Welsh   Tamworth   Danish Landrace

These are the main European breeds...

Pigs like eating, and get fat very quickly!

In the fields or in their pens, they snuffle about in the earth with their snouts, feasting on worms and snails, as well as roots and plants. Pigs love rolling in the mud to help them cool down. Their little eyes cannot see very far, but they have good ears. When they hear the farmer coming with a bucket of scraps, they snort with excitement! They will eat almost anything: potatoes, beetroot, cereals... and they drink over 10 litres of water each day.

A sow has a dozen piglets twice a year.

She is pregnant for about 114 days, or as the old saying goes: 'Three months, three weeks and three days!' At feeding time, she squeals to her piglets, and they all come rushing up, knocking each other over as they nuzzle up to her teats. A sow has twelve teats, and each piglet goes to its own particular one. Clever piglets choose the top ones, which give the most milk, so they grow up to be the strongest in the litter. If there are more than twelve piglets, the farmer will feed the weakest ones from a bottle.

Today we often keep pigs in cramped piggeries.

Pietrain   Large White   Gloucester Old Spot

...each one is a slightly different shape.

Saddleback   Curly coat   Berkshire

A tightly curled tail is a sign of good health.

This little pig went to market...

Many pigs are kept in large piggeries, more like factories than farms. The sows and their litters* are kept in special sties, the growing pigs in groups and the male pigs, the boars, on their own. Living in a tiny pen with hardly any room to move about, the pigs get fat three times more quickly than they would out in a field, but they may also get angry because they are unhappy. They are given their meals automatically, at the same time every day. If a pig is thirsty, it presses on a clapper and water runs into its trough. When the pigs weigh 100 kilos, at around five months old, they are taken to the abattoir* to be killed.

The meat from a pig is called pork. If it is smoked or cured, it is called ham or bacon. Some religions do not allow you to eat it. Some foods made from pork have a high fat* content, like paté or sausages.

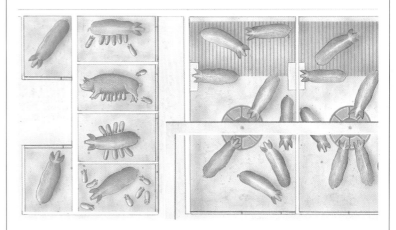

It's better for your health to cut the fat off chops or ham.

Roast pork, bacon, sausages, ham, chops, paté...

Salami sausage

Black Pudding

Italian Zampone

Sausages

Ham

Minced pork

Paté

Smoked Bacon

Cutlets

Pork roast: on the bone

and off the bone

Fillet half leg

Loin chops

Blade

Fillet

Knuckle

Belly

Hand and spring

Head

Trotters

How a butcher sees a pig.

Bath chaps

Streaky bacon

Blade

On small farms, in the past, it was a big day when the pig was killed and the meat prepared for winter stores. One pig would feed a family for a year. Now pigs are killed in an abattoir*.

A female rabbit is called a doe. She may have four litters* a year. She plucks the soft fur from her underside to line a nest for the babies.

A farm in Britain...

There are many different buildings on a farm. They may be dotted about the fields, ranged along a track or grouped around the farmyard. Each animal needs a shelter, and the farmer and his family need a house to live in, too. Cattle have their cowshed, pigs have their sties. There may be a barn with pens for the sheep in winter, a hen-house, and hutches if the farmer keeps rabbits... as well as sheds for the farm machinery, and barns where the hay and straw can be stacked.

Look at these three farms. They are all very different, but on each one the farmer is growing food for his animals – animals which in turn supply us with food.

another in Africa...

Sheep graze on grass in summer, but in winter they are often fed on root vegetables.

...and a third in North America, with its tall grain silo

Hens, geese, ducks and turkeys...

In an old-fashioned farmyard you might see lots of different birds scratching and pecking about. Hens give us eggs all the year round, and chicken is also a popular meat. A goose or a turkey is part of a traditional Christmas dinner. Roast duck is delicious, and so is guinea-fowl, although it is more unusual. Did you know that geese make good 'guard dogs'? They sound the alarm if a stranger comes near, hissing and cackling as loudly as they can!

Hens scratch out little hollows in the ground and groom themselves by flicking dust through their feathers. They hate getting wet!

Domestic geese stay on the farm and no longer migrate* to a warmer country in winter as their wild cousins do. Have you heard of a gaggle of geese? It is a flock, with a male, or gander, in charge. You can eat goose eggs, and geese are also reared for their meat. People have reared poultry birds for their eggs and meat since the Chinese began to keep chickens over 2,000 years ago.

Some of the eggs we eat come from battery hens. The birds are kept cooped up in rows of wire cages, in huge metal barns, with sloping floors for the eggs to roll down. It is a speedy, economical way to farm, but many people feel it is cruel and it can allow disease to spread among the birds. Hens roaming in the farm-yard are called free-range. They are fed on corn, meal and vegetable scraps, but they like worms and insects too. They also peck up tiny pieces of grit to help digest their food and make strong shells for their eggs. The hen-house is well-lit inside, because light stimulates the hens to lay. In winter, when the days are shorter, hens lay fewer eggs.

A cockerel may rule a roost of eight or ten hens.

What's in an egg?

Inside the shell there is a golden yolk with a transparent, sticky liquid, the white, all around it. If the cock and hen have mated, the egg will have been fertilized. If the hen sits on the egg and keeps it warm, a tiny spot on the yolk develops into a chick. The yolk and white are food for the chick until it hatches out. The eggs we eat never have a chick inside, because they are collected before the hen has a chance to sit on them. From time to time, a hen whose eggs are taken away will turn broody. The farmer lets her sit on some newly laid eggs and brood them until they hatch, twenty-one days later.

A chick hatches out.

The chick pecks at the shell from inside and cracks it open. When it hatches, it weighs only 30 to 40 grammes, the same as a large egg. In no time at all, its fluffy down dries out and it can walk and scratch for food on its own. By five months old, hens produce their first eggs and chickens are big enough to be eaten. Both eggs and chicken meat are high in proteins*, which help build and repair our muscles.

A sitting hen turns her eggs over regularly so that they are all kept equally warm.

Cows eat grass all day long.

In the old days, there were cattle on every farm. The bullocks used to pull the plough and the cows provided milk, for drinking and to make into butter and cheese. They also produced a calf each year, which the farmer could fatten and sell at market. Even the cow-dung was saved to spread on the fields as fertilizer*. There was definitely a rich smell about the farm in those days!

Cows eat grass, but they also like barley, maize, beetroot, soya...

Cows eat up to 60 kilos of grass a day.
In winter, when there is little pasture available, they also eat hay, cereals, beet and soya. They drink six large buckets full of water every day.

Chewing the cud, or ruminating
Grass is difficult to digest*, but the cow has developed a special way of coping. First, she pulls up the grass with her rough tongue and swallows it, hardly chewing it at all. The grass goes into her first and biggest stomach, to be softened by the juices there. Later, when the cow is resting, the food comes back into her mouth. She chews it once more, slowly and thoroughly, before swallowing it again to be digested in her second stomach. You can see how this works by following the different coloured arrows on the diagram.

During spring and summer, farmers in mountain areas take their herds up to high meadows, where the grass and clover are sweetest. Often the oldest cow in each herd is the leader.
In winter, most cows stay inside.
In the past, the cowshed used to be part of the farmhouse. The heat from the animals' bodies helped to keep the farmer and his family warm.

Dairy farmers produce milk from herds of dairy cows.

Up in the mountains, the cows graze on open pasture during spring and summer.

Nowadays, cows spend the winter in special cowsheds, or in barns which sometimes open out on yards or fields.

Cows must be milked every day.

On a farm, the cows are milked every morning and evening.
If the farmer is late, the cows get impatient and moo loudly.

When does a cow give milk?
When she has a calf. A cow is a mammal, which means she suckles her baby on milk. She carries the calf inside her for nine months. As soon as it is born, her udders fill with milk to feed it.

A cow which has not yet had a calf is called a heifer.

A cow has four or five calves in her life, and gives over 20,000 litres of milk: that's enough to fill two big tankers!

For ten months after her calf is born, a cow goes on giving around 20 litres of milk a day. She has a calf every year. By the age of six or seven, she is growing too old to have calves and she does not give so much milk. Scientists are always looking for ways to improve the milk that a cow yields. The type and quality of food she eats is very important.

Hardly anybody milks cows by hand nowadays.

Years ago, people used to drink milk just as it was, straight from the udder. But tiny bacteria* grow in untreated milk, and some of them can make you ill.
In the 19th century, a French scientist called Louis Pasteur discovered a way to destroy these bacteria.
The milk was heated to a high temperature for a few seconds, then quickly cooled down. Today, most milk is treated in this way. The process, called 'pasteurization' (after its inventor) keeps milk fresh for several days.

Bacteria seen much larger than life, under a microscope.

What happens at the dairy?

Most modern farmers use milking machines to help them milk their cows.
It only takes five minutes to milk each cow. The farmer gives her something to eat, so she will stand quietly while the job is done.
First the udders are wiped clean.
A milking machine sucks out the milk and takes it by pipe to a tank, where it is cooled to 4 degrees Celsius.
The cold stops bacteria* developing.
A refrigerated milk-tanker collects the milk each day and takes it to the dairy.

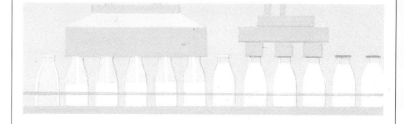

At the dairy, everything has to be very clean. The amount of cream in the milk is measured, and often some is skimmed off to make semi-skimmed milk. All milk contains very important proteins* and minerals*, like calcium*, which help your bones and teeth grow strong and healthy.

Milk is made into cream, butter, cheese and yoghurt.

People learned to make cheese thousands of years ago, when they began to keep flocks of dairy animals. Making cheese was a good way to use up old, stale milk. Cheese is made from the curdled milk of cows, sheep or goats. There are thousands of different kinds of cheese made the world over, each with a different taste and texture. The cream in milk is made into butter.

Have you ever poured a smooth, thick stream of cream over your strawberries? **Cream is the richest part of milk.** In this old-fashioned dairy they are making cream and butter. A separator (1) spins round fast to separate the cream from the milk. Then the cream is tipped into a churn (2), where it is beaten. It turns yellow and becomes firm as specks of fat* in the cream stick together.

Double cream and whipped cream

As the butter forms, a thin liquid called buttermilk runs off it. It takes 22 litres of milk to make one kilo of butter. If salt is added, butter keeps for longer. In the old days, butter was left in pats, or shaped in pretty wooden moulds (3). Today it is wrapped in paper or put in plastic containers.
Butter contains vitamin A, which helps prevent infection and is good for our teeth, skin, bones and eyes. Some doctors think that you should not eat too much butter – it is high in the sort of fats which can harm our health.

There are thousands of different sorts of cheese.

Roquefort,
France: sheep's milk

Stilton, England:
cow's milk

Feta, Greece:
sheep's milk

Edam, Holland:
cow's milk

Cheese can be hard, like Cheddar, or soft, like Brie. Most British cheeses are made from cows' milk. Each originally came from a different region, like Cheshire or Leicester, with its own special recipe. A Stilton cheese has blue veins in it, because it is treated with a special mould and left to mature for 6 to 9 months. French cheeses are famous world-wide and there are more than 400 of them.

Traditional cheese-making

Different cheeses are made in different ways, but they all start off with curdling.

The milk is warmed, and then 'starter' is added to make the milk go sour. Next, rennet, from a calf's stomach, is put in to make the milk clot and set. The milk separates into curds and whey.

Swiss Emmenthal is matured at 22 to 27 degrees Celsius. Bubbles of carbon dioxide build up inside the cheese, forming the holes we see when it is cut.

The solid curds are put into a bag so that the liquid whey drains off.

Next, hard cheeses have to be pressed. Some, like Cheddar, are mixed with salt first. Then they are put in a large, round mould, and pressed more and more tightly.

Finally, the cheese is left to mature. This is when the flavour of each cheese develops.

Cheddar is usually kept for about five months, but mature Cheddar is kept for at least ten months and tastes much stronger.

A cellar of maturing cheeses

The oceans are a rich source of food.

Sardine   Whiting

Mackerel

Herring

People have been eating fish and shellfish for thousands of years.
We know because seashells, fish bones and fish hooks have been found on ancient rubbish tips that may be 10,000 years old.
There are thousands of different kinds of fish in the sea, and many of them are good to eat. Some like to live in the open sea, some prefer the shoreline or the sea-bed. Fishermen have to know where each kind likes to live and feed, so they have a good chance of catching them.

Deep sea fishing

Special boats called trawlers go far out to sea for weeks, sometimes months, at a time. Cod, sole and plaice are pulled up from the bottom in a huge, funnel-shaped net, called a trawl, which drags behind the boat. Herring and mackerel are caught near the surface in drift nets, which hang in the water like curtains.

The biggest trawlers are like floating factories.
The fish have to be gutted, cleaned and frozen quickly on board ship, or they go bad.

Fish and shellfish are the harvest of the sea.

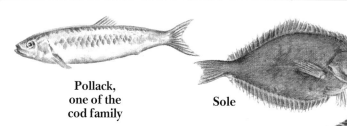

Pollack, one of the cod family

Sole

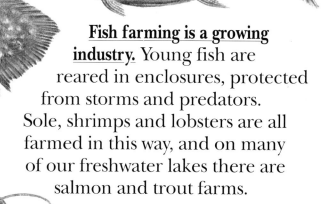

Tuna

Skate

Bass, pollack and sea-bream live close to shore. They are caught on a line with hooks all along it. Boats that go fishing for tuna carry a boom, a sort of long pole with several fishing lines running from one end of it.

Fish farming is a growing industry. Young fish are reared in enclosures, protected from storms and predators. Sole, shrimps and lobsters are all farmed in this way, and on many of our freshwater lakes there are salmon and trout farms.

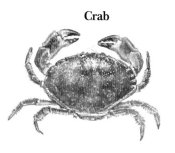

Crab

Shrimp

Lobster

Mussels

Winkles

Oysters

You can find lots of interesting things along the seashore at low tide!
Beachcombers copy professional fishermen and use shovels, rakes and knives to gather the shellfish that are left behind when the tide goes out: clams and scallops, cockles and winkles. Some shellfish bury themselves in the sand or mud. Others, like mussels and limpets, cling to rocks.
For too long we have taken the riches of the sea for granted. Some species are in danger from over-fishing.
Now laws control when and where fishing can take place, as well as the amount of fish each nation's fishing fleet can take from the sea.

Mussel and oyster farms are now becoming more common too.
The young larvae are fixed to a suitable rough surface below the tide mark where they can grow.
All fish is good for us, and it's delicious too! It gives us magnesium, phosphorus, vitamins*, protein* and oils.

Mussel and oyster farms have been set up along stretches of coast which are exposed at low tide.

Salt is everywhere –
in the sea, in the soil,
even in the rain.
Salt is vital for our health:
it helps to regulate
how much water our body contains.
Where does the salt we eat come from?
It is naturally present in many of our foods.
But the extra salt we add to food has been
extracted from the sea, or from underground.
Before fridges, people used salt to preserve
food. Salted meat or fish keeps for a long time.

**Ever since prehistoric times, people have
collected salt from the sea.**
It was the Romans who first built salt-pans.
Seawater circulates very slowly along
channels through a series of shallow pools.
The sun's heat makes the water evaporate,
and the salt is left behind.

When the salt has formed crystals, the salt-
maker collects it in a pile and pushes
it towards the dike. The large, grey crystals
fall to the bottom, leaving the tiny,
white crystals gleaming on top.

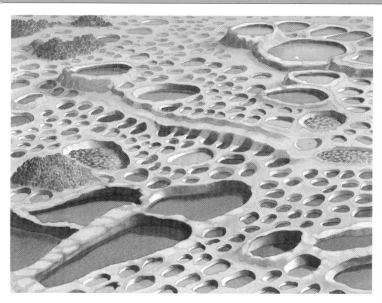

In some African deserts, salt-lakes come and go with the rainy and dry seasons, year after year. When the lakes evaporate, they leave a crust of salt over the land.

In Niger, the ground is very salty, and the spring water that collects in natural basins is very salty, too. The local people pour it into moulds made from the hollowed-out trunks of palm trees. When the water has evaporated, they break the moulds and are left with loaves of salt.

An open-cast salt mine in Mali. Salt is cut into slabs each weighing 60 kilos, and then transported by camel.

In other African countries, like Mali, the people cut the salty crust on the ground into blocks, which they prise up with long sticks. The blocks are then shaped into slabs and carried by camel to the nearest market. Salt is very precious to people and animals who live in the desert. It helps their bodies replace the salt they lose through sweating in the heat.

Salt was once an expensive object of trade. It could be exchanged for slaves or gold, and there were even coins made of salt. Roman soldiers were paid partly in salt, and now when people talk of earning a 'salary', they are using a word that comes from the Latin for salt.

<u>The salt dug up from mines</u> was left behind by the seas which once covered the Earth, millions of years ago.

The first salt-miners

Each time the Earth's crust shifted, the salt was buried deeper under rock and soil. The first salt mines were dug about 3,000 years ago. For people living far from the sea, salt mines were a great discovery. Men went down into the mines on ropes, used picks to dig out huge blocks of salt and carried them up on their backs. Later, horses were used to bring the salt up in barrels.

The heads of these picks are made of bronze. Oil-lamps hanging from the walls lit up the mines.

People discovered the many uses of salt a long time ago.

Meat and fish steeped in salt keep for several months, because salt absorbs the water in food and dries it out. It also destroys the bacteria* that make food rot. Nowadays, for a healthy diet, we are advised to avoid salty foods, and not add much salt to our food.

The Egyptians used to pluck and dress the ducks they had killed, then pack them in salt.

The Scandinavian countries of northern Europe had no salt mines, and not enough sunshine to evaporate the water in salt-pans. They had to buy salt from France, Italy and Portugal, and pay for it in gold! The salt came by boat over the sea and up the rivers and then overland on mules. The salt trade was worth a lot of money, and at times wars were waged because of it.

Salt was also used as a medicine.

Now almost every country in the world, apart from Scandinavia and Japan, produces its own salt. Most of the salt we eat is rock-salt, dug out of mines. The biggest producers in the world are the United States and China.

In a modern mine, salt is extracted on a massive scale. One explosion can bring down 500 tonnes of salt at a time. The pieces are loaded on to tip-trucks and carried off to be broken up and crushed by machines, then washed, sieved and put into packets.

Bees work hard to make honey.

Do you like a spoonful of sweet, sticky honey on your bread? For thousands of years, people have enjoyed eating honey. They learned to look for it in the hollow trees where wild bees nest.
Beekeepers keep bees in little wooden houses called beehives, so they can collect the honey more easily. Thousands of bees may live in one hive. Most of them are females, and each has a job to do.

| Lime | Acacia | Chestnut | Fir | Thyme |

Each type of flower gives the honey a different flavour.

There is one queen in each hive.

She lays eggs that hatch into white larvae which eventually turn into young bees. A few bees are drones, male bees whose job is to fertilize the queen. All the others are female workers. They look after the larvae, clean the hive, collect nectar* and pollen* from the flowers, to make wax and honey.

A worker bee's body has special tools. Its long probing tongue is used to suck up nectar from the flowers. The hairs on its back legs collect the pollen. It has strong upper jaws, or mandibles which it uses to soften the wax and build cells where the larvae are cared for, and where the honey is kept.

The bee fixes the pollen to sacs on its back legs.

Bees make honey from nectar*.

In the hive, worker-bees turn the sugary liquid into a sticky paste by beating their wings over it. Then they chew it up. Some is mixed with pollen* to feed the larvae. The rest is stored in cells which are stopped up with wax: this is the honey the beekeeper collects.

The beekeeper takes the roof off the hive and lifts out the frames of honey. He scrapes off the top covering of wax, then spins them very fast in a machine called a separator, to make the honey run out. In a single season, he may collect 35 large jars full of honey. But he always leaves enough for the bees to live on through the winter.

Every leafy plant contains sugar.

Do you like the sweet taste of sugar? Did you know that every green plant's cells contain chlorophyll? It is what makes leaves green. Chlorophyll absorbs the sun's rays and combines them with water and the carbon dioxide gas in the air to make sugar. Sugar is stored in the fruit, sap, stalk, roots and leaves of a plant.

Sugar cane is particularly rich in sugar.

Sugar cane is a kind of reed which grows in tropical countries, where the climate is hot and humid. Inside the sugar cane is a firm, white pulp where the sugar is stored. It is deliciously sweet and juicy to chew on.

Planting sugar cane

Short sections of sugar cane, called setts, are planted in trenches.

They take root and send up a shoot. Eighteen months later, the canes are cut. Every year for five or six years, fresh canes are cut from the old ones. Then it is time to plant new setts.

Harvesting the cane

When the canes are 4 or 5 metres high, they are ready to be cut. Today, they are often harvested by machines.

In many places, however, the canes are still cut by hand with a long knife called a machete. It's very hard work! The canes are picked up and taken to the sugar factory as quickly as possible, because as soon as they are cut, they begin to lose their sweetness.

The sugar mill

In the past, canes were crushed in a mill. As the mill ground them down, a dark brown liquid was squeezed out, full of little bits of leaf and stem. Now, in most parts of the world, modern sugar factories use machines, but still follow traditional methods. The juice is collected in vats, and heated up.

The sugar used to be poured into cone-shaped moulds while it was still hot.

The brown juice is boiled, and dirt and impurities are removed. The juice thickens as water evaporates.

After a while, sugar crystals begin to appear.
Brown sugar crystals are turned into white ones in a refinery, where the crystals are melted down and cleaned again. The whiter the sugar, the more refined it is.

Two hundred years ago, sugar was rare and expensive in Europe, because it had to be brought by ship from far away.

Sugar used to be a luxury.

From the 18th century onwards in Europe, chocolate and coffee were becoming increasingly popular, and more and more sugar was in demand to sweeten them.

In 1807, England was at war with France, and all overseas trade came to a standstill. **Ports were blocked, and the ships bringing the sugar cane could not get through!** The English had developed a sweet tooth and so had the French. How would they manage now?

The answer was there all the time in the ground: sugar-beet!

This root vegetable grows well in mild climates like ours. As it grows, it stores sugar in its thick, white root. People had been experimenting for a long time with carrots, grapes and even potatoes, to see which would produce the most sugar. Sugar-beet was found to give the best results. A French chemist, Benjamin Delessert discovered, in 1802, a way of extracting the sugar from sugar-beet in large quantities. The Emperor Napoleon was so pleased that he ordered huge fields of sugar-beet to be planted, and soon the French had all the sugar they wanted.

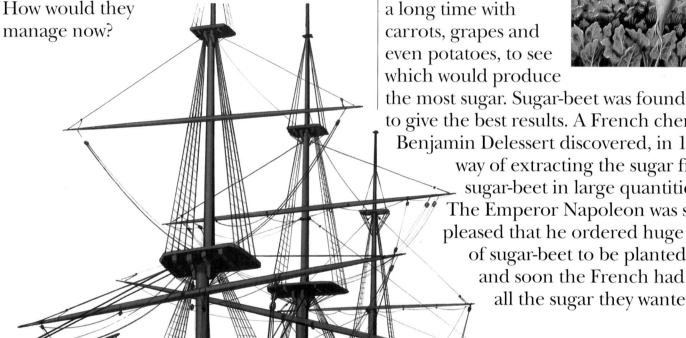

Now there is sugar in many of the foods we eat.

The sugar-beet seed is planted in spring. By May, clumps of green leaves are showing above the ground. In the warmth of the summer sun, sugar begins to collect in the root as it grows larger.
All through the autumn months, the beets are harvested. Special machines cut off the leaves and haul the beets out of the ground. They are quickly taken to the nearby factory, where they are treated to extract the sugar.

From September until Christmas, these factories are at work day and night. In Britain, half the sugar we eat comes from sugar-beet which we grow here. The rest is made from sugar cane which we buy from other countries.

Three hundred years ago, sugar was a luxury, an expensive treat kept for special occasions! Nowadays, you find it in many of the foods you eat, from baked beans to yoghurt!

Sweet things like lollipops, ice-cream, cakes, fizzy drinks and sweets are all made from sugar. If you are playing lots of sport, sugar can give you a quick burst of energy when you are tired. But too much sugar rots your teeth and makes you fat.

Granulated sugar is made up of little crystals. It can be shaped into sugar lumps, ground down into caster sugar, or ground even more finely into powdery icing sugar. Sugar candy is made of larger crystals which take longer to form.

Did you know that chocolate grows on trees?

You can eat it, mix it with milk and drink it, make ice-creams with it...

But just what is chocolate? Chocolate comes from the beans of the cocoa tree, a plant which keeps its leaves and flowers all year round. The flowers ripen into pods, and inside each one are thirty or forty seeds, wrapped in a soft white pulp. These are the cocoa beans.

The flowers of the cocoa tree grow straight out of the trunk and main branches, and ripen into pods.

Cocoa trees like hot, damp climates.

They are grown throughout the tropical regions of Africa and South America. When they grow wild in the forest, they can be 10 to 15 metres high, but in plantations they are cut back to keep them about 4 or 5 metres high, to make it easier to harvest the pods.

When they are ripe, the pods are a beautiful red or orange colour. Once they are picked, they are sliced in half. The beans are taken out of the white pulp by hand.

Who first tried chocolate as a drink?

The recipe comes from Mexico, where the Aztecs*, the local Indians, drank it. The first European to taste it was the Spanish general, Cortes, in the 16th century. The Aztec Emperor Montezuma welcomed him with a present of cocoa pods, and offered him a drink made from cocoa beans.

Chocolate was first used to make a bitter drink.

The Aztecs of Mexico first of all grilled the cocoa beans, then crushed them and mixed them with maize flour, pepper, vanilla and water. It made a nourishing but rather bitter drink. Cortes liked it so much that he sent a boat back to Spain packed entirely with cocoa beans.

The Aztecs* used the dried beans for trading. Ten cocoa beans, for example, might buy a rabbit.

Cooks at the Spanish court thought the drink should be less bitter, so they added sugar instead of pepper. What a success! The new drink became fashionable among the rich and elegant, and every noble lord wanted a chocolate-maker as part of his household.

The fashion of drinking chocolate spread across Europe.
Doctors recommended it to their patients as a tonic. Then, in the 19th century, Meunier, Lindt, Fry and Cadbury were among the first chocolate manufacturers to begin to make blocks of chocolate in their factories.

Fresh cocoa beans don't taste at all like chocolate! They are very bitter.

How do cocoa beans come to taste of chocolate?
Once they have been picked out of their pulp, they are left for a week in large chests, covered with damp banana leaves. Every day, they are given a good stir. They ferment* and turn brown. It is then that they begin to take on their special taste.

Once they have fermented, they are spread out on large trays to dry in the sun for a week or two. The workers turn them over regularly to make sure they all dry out properly. If it rains, the trays can slide back on runners under cover. If the beans crack when you squeeze them, they are properly dry and will keep for a long time without going mouldy.

Now they are ready to be packed into sacks and put on board ship for export.

There is a long journey ahead for the cocoa beans before they reach the chocolate factories.

Cocoa is grown in Brazil and in Ecuador, in Ghana, Nigeria, Cameroon and the Ivory Coast. Cocoa is a cash-crop* which is exported to Europe and North America, where the beans are turned into chocolate.

Cocoa trees grow in hot countries, mainly in West Africa, South America, Asia and Malaysia.

In the chocolate factory

First the beans are sorted and cleaned. Then they are grilled, to crack open the shells and to bring out their full flavour. Machines crush them into a bitter paste. Then the paste is pressed very hard to squeeze out all the fat; this is called cocoa butter. To make chocolate, cocoa paste, cocoa butter and sugar are mixed together and stirred for two or three days without stopping. Later, dried milk powder, raisins, nuts or puffed grains of rice can be added to make all sorts of different kinds of chocolate bars.

Coffee: a drink to wake you up!

The story goes that coffee was discovered in Yemen by some shepherds. They noticed that their goats became lively when they had eaten the red berries from a particular bush. The shepherds tried the berries themselves, and found they could not sleep! The plant was, of course, a coffee bush.

A ripe coffee berry looks like a little red cherry. Inside are two green beans, which turn brown once they are roasted.

The big coffee plantations

Today, coffee is grown in most tropical countries, especially in Africa and South America. The biggest crops of all come from Brazil.

Right up until the 19th century, some plantations were worked by slaves brought over from Africa to look after the coffee plants, water the bushes and pick the berries.

Coffee is a sensitive plant. Too much or too little rain, or the cold, can destroy a whole crop.

Harvesting coffee

When the berries are ripe, they are picked by hand, one by one, or pulled off the bushes using special combs. Once gathered into large baskets, the berries are dried and boiled to release the coffee beans.

The green coffee bean does not smell of anything. It only goes brown and begins to have that special coffee smell after it has been roasted.

Each kind of coffee has a different flavour: Arabica, from Brazil and Colombia, is the most popular. African Robusta has a more bitter taste.

Tea: a drink to revive you!

Grown-ups also enjoy tea. Like coffee, tea contains a chemical called caffeine, which helps keep you going for a while when you are tired. Tea also comes from a plant which grows in hot climates. The Chinese first noticed that tea leaves steeped in boiling water made a delicious drink. Drinking tea has been a custom in Japan, too, for thousands of years, and has developed into a special ceremony.

Tea did not appear in Europe until the 16th century. Dutch merchants travelled to Japan and brought back the first chests of tea. It was not long before people were drinking it all over Europe, but it became especially popular in Britain. It was the British who planted the huge tea plantations in India and Sri Lanka. Since that time, India has become the largest tea producer in the world.

Tea leaves are picked by hand, one by one.
The best tea is made from pekoe: the youngest, most tender leaves growing at the tip of the stem.

The next four or five leaves along the stalk are worth picking too, but the others are all too tough. Harvesting is carried out all year long. The leaves are spread out, dried, turned and heated. Gradually they go brown. Sometimes tea leaves are flavoured with flowers like jasmine, or orange-blossom.

Herbs and spices add exciting flavours to our cooking.

Have you ever walked into the kitchen and sniffed the peppery smell of gingerbread baking in the oven? Ginger is one of the spices that make your nose twitch. The jars of brownish powder labelled cinnamon, ginger or nutmeg may look unexciting, but the spices they contain add strong, warming flavours to our food. Herbs also give extra taste to our cooking. Each has its own special smell and flavour. Herbs may be used fresh or dried. We use vegetable oil to help cook or add a dressing to our food. Oil is a rich, clear liquid that comes from certain plants.

These are some common spices:

A stem from a pepper-plant showing its seeds, the peppercorns.

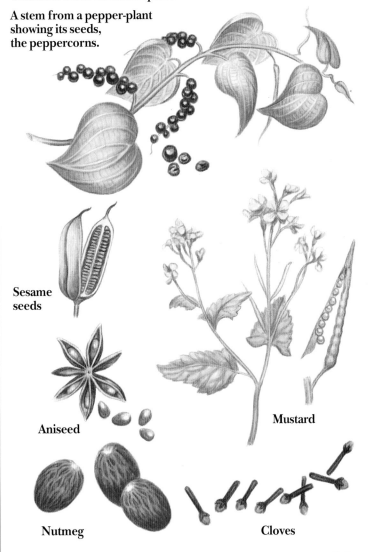

Sesame seeds

Aniseed

Mustard

Nutmeg

Cloves

Most of the spices we use come from the East.

The first spice to be used in Europe was pepper. It came from India. Ginger is the root of a plant which grows in tropical climates. Cinnamon comes from rolls of bark, and cloves are dried, unopened buds from the clove tree. For hundreds of years, these spices, along with nutmeg and sesame seeds, were all very rare and expensive products. During the Middle Ages, only rich nobles could afford them. It was not easy to keep food fresh, and the strong flavour of spices helped disguise the taste of stale meat and fish. Many spices were also used as medicines.

Cinnamon

Fresh herbs:

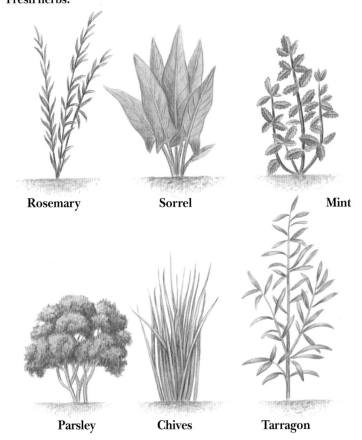

Rosemary   Sorrel   Mint

Parsley   Chives   Tarragon

Oil is pressed from the fruits or seeds of various plants.

Olives are the fruit of the olive tree.

We can grow herbs in the garden, or in a pot on the windowsill.

A few sprigs of thyme, rosemary or basil, or a bay leaf, will give a delicious flavour to any soup, fish or meat. Parsley, chives and tarragon can be finely chopped and sprinkled on salads and other dishes. Cooks have been using all these herbs since the Middle Ages. Like spices, they can also used as medicines.

Some plants give us oil.

Oil is made from the crushed seeds of certain plants. Some, such as cotton, soya and peanuts, need hot climates to grow. Others, like rape, sunflowers or maize, will grow in cooler countries. Coconuts and olives give us oil, as well.

How is the oil produced?

The outer husks are removed, then the seeds are crushed and heated gently to get rid of the excess water they contain.

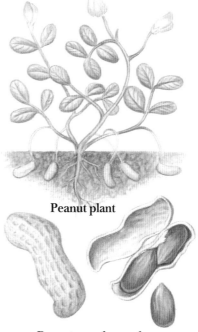

Peanut plant

Peanuts are the seeds.

Then the seeds go through a press which reduces them to a pulp and releases their oil, which at this stage is very thick. The oil must be refined and distilled to make it easier for us to digest.

Weight for weight, oil contains more calories than any other food. Oil gives us energy as well as many of the minerals* and vitamins* we need to grow. Sunflower, peanut and soya oil are used to make margarine. Margarine can be used in place of butter, although it has a different taste. Certain margarines have less harmful fats* than butter, and are thought by some doctors to be better for you.

Rape

Sunflowers are laden with seeds. They always turn their heads to face the sun, and this is how they got their name.

Games and activities, intriguing facts, a quiz, sayings, a glossary, followed by the index

■ Did you know?

In many countries, bread is baked for special occasions. Bread can be crisp like a biscuit, or soft and spongey.

Chinese New Year bread

German New Year's Pretzel

Easter Plait

Pilgrim's bread

The croissant is a kind of soft, flaky bread made in the shape of a crescent. It was first made in 1683, in Vienna in Austria. The city had been besieged by the Turks, but their army was beaten and they fled, leaving behind large stocks of coffee. A Polish man decided to open a café, and he asked a baker to make something to serve with the coffee. The baker made croissants to commemorate the victory, because of the crescent on the Turkish flag.

French bread goes into space!

Special sticks of French bread were made for the astronauts to take with them on the space shuttle Columbia in 1985. They were special because they didn't make any crumbs!

In many countries round the Mediterranean, a special sweet bread almost like a cake is made at Easter time. It is decorated with a red painted egg.

In parts what used to be called Yugoslavia, if a boy is in love with a girl, he gives her a little heart made of bread.

Every country, every region, bakes its own type of bread. Have you ever seen these breads?

Soft rolls or baps

Naan bread

Pretzel

Pitta bread

Crusty roll

Baton

Biscotte

Crispbreads

Brioche

Multigrain loaf

Pasta was invented by the Chinese. In 1271, Marco Polo set out from Venice to explore the East. It was twenty-four years before he returned from his travels in China, Mongolia and India. Among other things, he brought back with him the recipe for pasta. Now, pasta is one of the specialities of Italian cooking.

Sandwiches were the invention of an Englishman, Lord Sandwich, who was a very keen card-player. One day in 1762, he was so involved in a game that he refused to stop for dinner. He asked for a slice of meat between two pieces of bread. It was the first sandwich!

Canned food was the brainwave of a Parisian, called Nicolas Appert. The French government was offering a prize to anyone who could find a way of preserving food for the troops when they were away on a long campaign. Appert perfected a method of sterilization: first he sealed the food in a glass jar, and then heated it to a high temperature, at least 100 degrees Celsius, to destroy any bacteria*. The experiment was a success. In 1810, Appert won the prize.

■ Did you know?

The creamiest types of milk are **Channel Island** and **full-cream** milk: you can clearly see the layer of cream on top of the milk in the bottle. **Semi-skimmed** milk has had some cream removed, and **skimmed** milk contains virtually none. **Unpasteurized** milk comes straight from the farm. If it is boiled for 10 minutes, it will keep for up to two days in the fridge. **Fresh pasteurized** milk shows a sell-by date. It will keep, unopened, for 6 days in the fridge. **Sterilized milk and U.H.T. (ultra-heat-treated) milk** is flash-heated to a very high temperature, 132 degrees Celsius, for just over a second. Both types will keep, unopened, for at least three months.

The first cookery book was written by a Roman called Apicius, who lived in the 1st century B.C. He wrote down the ingredients for each recipe, but not their quantities! He invented dishes using such delicacies as larks' and flamingos' tongues, camels' fetlocks and sows' udders. He also gave several recipes for cakes and sauces.

Do people drink only cows' milk?

No, we also drink goats' milk, sheep's milk and, in certain countries, milk from horses, asses and camels.

Indian buffaloes

Female zebu

In Asia, Tibetans drink yaks' milk.

The Lapps in Finland, Sweden and Norway need the milk from the great herds of reindeer they follow.

The Tuareg people of Africa move their herds from place to place to find grazing for their animals.

The Indians of the Andes mountains drink llamas' milk.

Plates

In Europe, our early ancestors used to help themselves and eat straight from the main cooking pot. Then in the Middle Ages, the porringer appeared: it was an individual bowl for soup. Bread and meat were eaten from thick pieces of wood, called trenchers. Although rich people used plates sooner, they were not common until the end of the 18th century.

Knives

Right up to the end of the 16th century, people had their own knives, which they took with them if they went to dine with a friend. These knives had sharp points, for spearing the meat.

Forks

For a long time, people used to eat with their fingers. By the Middle Ages, noblemen used forks which had just two prongs, but they were a luxury, like a table cloth! Forks, glasses and plates did not become widely used until the end of the 18th century.

Breakfast

Twenty years ago, breakfast was a big meal. Some people still like a full English breakfast with cereal, fruit juice, eggs and bacon, toast and tea.

■ Did you know?

Snails have long been considered a delicacy. Romans fattened them on snail-farms. In the Middle Ages, they were fried with onions. The French cook them with butter and garlic.

Pigs hunt for truffles.
A truffle is a sort of mushroom with a strong smell. Truffles grow underground, mostly under oak trees. Farmers use sows, with their fine sense of smell, to root in the earth and uncover the truffles. Paté flavoured with truffles is a luxury.

Pigs can be pets!
In Papua New Guinea, a big island to the north of Australia, people treat baby pigs as pets, just as you would a dog or cat. The pigs live in the house with the family, and are taken about on leads. The more pigs a family has, the richer it is. But unfortunately for the pig, when it is fully grown it is killed and eaten at a big feast.

■ Quiz

There is one correct answer to each question. Have a go with your friends! You will find the answers on page 69.

1. What is Roquefort cheese made from?
a) sheep's milk
b) cow's milk
c) goat's milk

2. Which country is the largest tea producer in the world?
a) China
b) India
c) Japan

3. What is couscous made from?
a) ground-up maize
b) ground-up rice
c) ground-up wheat

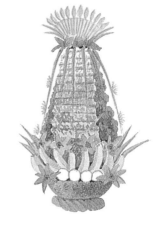

Rice is very important in Asia. When farmers on the island of Bali, in Indonesia, pray for a good harvest, they offer beautiful and intricately decorated rice-cakes to their gods.

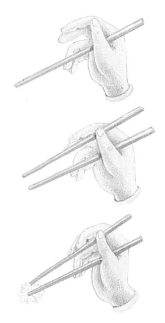

How do you eat with chopsticks? Hold the lower chopstick steady between your thumb and third finger. The top chopstick, held between the tip of your thumb and your index finger, picks up the rice and presses it against the lower chopstick. Rice which sticks together a little after it has been cooked is easier to pick up.

■ Did you know?

Who first discovered sugar?

The Hindus in India! They found a way of making sugar crystals

from the juice of a sort of wild cane.

Our word sugar comes from their Sanskrit word 'sarkara', meaning sugar crystals. Alexander the Great, king of Macedonia, discovered wild sugar-cane on an expedition to India in the 4th century B.C.

The Greeks then began to import sugar. Merchants brought sugar to northern Europe in the 11th century.

In Britain we eat, on average, 36-7 kilos of sugar each, every year. That's probably more than you weigh! A hundred years ago, sugar was still rare and expensive, and you could only buy 30 grammes at a time.

■ Quiz

4. Each day, you should drink at least...
a) 3 glasses of water
b) 10 glasses of water
c) 25 glasses of water

5. Which of these would be the best breakfast?
a) a glass of cola and some sweets
b) sausages, a slice of white toast and a cup of coffee
c) cereal or wholemeal toast, fruit juice and a yoghurt

6. What are vitamins?
a) foods that are high in calories
b) tiny particles that are found in water
c) elements in our food that are essential for good health

Answers: 1a 2b 3c 4b 5c 6c

There's more to salt than flavouring food!

Long ago, people thought it had miraculous healing powers. In the days of the Ancient Greeks and Romans, salt was sprinkled on houses to ward off illness. Whether as an ointment, a powder, or a tonic, doctors would prescribe salt to ease all sorts of aches and pains: wasp stings, heart pain, tooth decay, coughs and even laziness! Sprains and pulled muscles were strapped up with poultices made of nettles mixed with salt.

Salt-cellar from the past **Salt box**

Today, salt can still be used as a remedy for many ailments.

If your feet ache or are swollen, try soaking them in salted water. If your throat feels sore, gargle with warm, salted water. If you feel tired, a hot bath with salt in it may help you to relax. But be careful! Doctors think too much salt can make your blood pressure rise and put a strain on your heart.

In winter, salt is spread on roads to melt snow and ice.

■ Making little animals out of marzipan.

For the marzipan you will need:

250 grammes of icing sugar
250 grammes of ground almonds
2 egg whites
food colourings (red, green and yellow)

Mix together the icing sugar and ground almonds in a bowl.

Add the egg whites and mix again into a firm paste that is easy to work with. Divide the paste into three or four balls and add a few drops of different colouring to each one.

To make the model animals you will need:

stoned prunes and dates, glacé cherries, almonds, walnuts, hazelnuts, currants and a few sticks of liquorice.

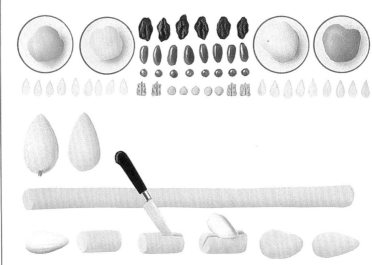

Marzipan mice: Roll some marzipan into a sausage shape and cut it into pieces, each one a little bigger than an almond. Split each piece down the middle with a knife and push an almond inside; then model the marzipan around the nut in the shape of a mouse's body. Use two almonds for its ears, and liquorice for its eyes and tail.

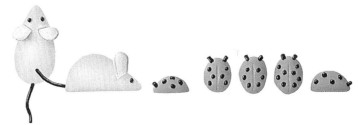

Ladybirds: the body is a hazelnut wrapped in marzipan; the spots and antennae are made of liquorice.

Owls and snails: Model the owl's head and body from marzipan. Make the wings from a date split in two, use a piece of cherry for the beak, liquorice for the eyes and ear-tufts, and currants for the feet.
A snail shell is made of a walnut shell, stuck on a roll of marzipan for the body.
You can make a butterfly using dates split in half for the wings, or a hedgehog from a ball of marzipan studded with currants.
Use your imagination to make some other animals!

■ Eggs in their nests:

Four large potatoes

8 eggs

50 grammes of butter

Salt and pepper

You will need a grown-up to help you.
1. Collect together all the things you need for the recipe.
2. Set the oven to 200 degrees C, gas mark 6.
3. Scrub the potatoes and wrap each one in silver foil.
4. Bake the potatoes in the oven for an hour and a half.
5. Melt the butter in a saucepan.
6. While the potatoes are still hot, cut them in half and scoop out the centre of each to make a nest.
7. Lay them in a baking dish. Pour some butter into each nest and break an egg into it.
8. Sprinkle with salt and pepper, then put the dish back in the oven until the eggs are cooked.

■ Did you know you can print with potatoes?

Here's how you do it!

ABCD

First, collect together all the things you will need.

To make the stamps:
a few potatoes
a knife with a sharp point –
but ask a grown-up to help you!
a pencil

And for the printing:
some tubes of paint or a bottle of ink
a small, shallow tin
some blotting paper
sheets of paper to print on
some old newspapers to protect the table
an apron to protect you!

You could print a frieze to decorate the top of your writing paper, or invitations to your birthday party.
You might like to print your initials on the first page of some of your favourite books.

First you have to make the stamps:
1. Cut a potato in half.
2. Draw a simple, clear design onto it, then cut round it with a knife. The design should stand out in relief. Remember to make any letters the wrong way round!

To print:
3. Put a pad of blotting paper in the tin and soak it thoroughly with ink or paint.
4. Press the potato, face down, onto the pad, then onto the sheet of paper you have chosen.

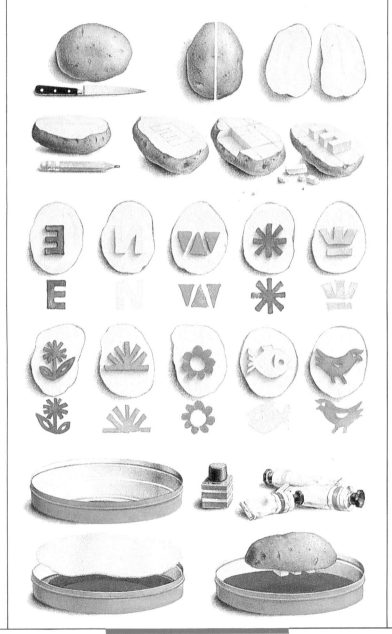

Radish seeds

Compost

Pebbles

■ Radishes in pots!

Put a few pebbles into a pot, then some compost. Plant 3 or 4 radish seeds. Lightly cover them with

compost and water well. Place the pot on a light windowsill. Water it every couple of days. After about a month, your radishes will be ready to eat!

If you are growing the long type of radish, make sure you plant the seeds deep enough so that the radishes don't grow twisted.

■ Glossary

Abattoir: a place where animals are taken to be killed for their meat. There are rules which must be followed so that the animals do not suffer too much stress or pain.

Additive: anything which is added to food. Additives can be substances which add colour to or improve the flavour of food (colourings or flavourings) or they can be preservatives, which help the food keep longer. Labels on food packaging tell you which additives are in the food.

Aztecs: an American Indian people who settled in what we now know as Mexico. During the 14th century, they built up a powerful and sophisticated empire. They were conquered by the Spanish after 1521.

Bacteria: microscopic organisms found almost everywhere. Some are harmful, and cause disease. Others perform useful functions in a healthy body, helping to break down waste products. Bacteria are essential in many food processes, such as making butter, cheese or yoghurt.

Calcium: an essential mineral our bodies need to build strong bones and teeth.

Carbohydrate: a compound of carbon, hydrogen and oxygen found in food, which produces energy. Sugar and starch are carbohydrates.

Cash-crop: a crop grown solely for sale, rather than the farmer's own use.

Corn dolly: a small decoration made of dried corn stalks with the ear of the grain still intact. They are often intricately woven, and used to be hung around the farmhouse to bring good luck.

Cultivate: to develop a plant using farming or gardening techniques.

Digestion: the process by which we break down food inside us, releasing its energy and goodness.

Domestication: pigs, cows, sheep and goats were once wild animals. Man has domesticated them over the centuries. Horses were first domesticated four thousand years ago.

Fat: a vital source of vitamins and energy.

Eating too many saturated fats in meats and dairy products is thought to be unhealthy; vegetable fats are better for you.

Fermentation: bacteria and yeast break down the sugars in food. The process is used in baking bread, and producing cheese, yoghurt and wine.

Fertilizer: anything added to soil to help plants grow better – animal manures or chemical fertilizers.

Fibre: essential to healthy digestion. Fibre is in many unprocessed foods, and in all fruit and vegetables.

Germination: This takes place when a seed has the right conditions of light, moisture and temperature. A root goes down into the soil and a shoot goes up – growth has begun.

Harrow: a heavy frame with iron teeth, pulled behind a tractor. It is used to break up clods of earth on ploughed land, or to cover the seeds after sowing.

Incas: South American Indian people of Peru, whose empire was at its

height in the 15th century. Their Emperor was known as the Inca, and people believed he was descended from the Sun. The Inca civilization was destroyed by the Spanish in the 1530s.

Litter: a brood of young animals all born to one mother at the same time.

Migration: some animals, birds, fish and even insects make long and difficult journeys in search of food, or to avoid cold and wet. These seasonal journeys, which happen year after year, are called migration.

Mineral: an inorganic substance such as iron, calcium or phosphorus which our bodies need for healthy growth.

Nectar: a sugary liquid produced by flowers. As insects drink it, they pick up pollen and carry it from one plant to another so flowers are fertilized.

Pollen: powder produced by flowers which plays a part in plant reproduction.

Protein: an essential nutrient in the food of all animals.
to Prune: to trim or cut back a plant to encourage vigorous, healthy growth. Fruit trees, for instance, are pruned regularly so they produce plenty of fruit.

Seed-drill: a machine that is pulled behind a tractor, and is used for sowing seeds. The seeds run out of a hopper and down through tubes into the furrows,

which are made by a set of blades attached in front. A harrow is drawn along behind to cover the seeds with soil.

Staple food: the basic food eaten by the people of a particular area. The staple food in Italy could be said to be pasta, whereas in China it is rice.

Vegetarian: a person who does not eat meat or fish for reasons of health, principles or religion. Vegans eat no animal products at all and often do not wear leather.

Vitamins: substances found in foods, especially when raw, which are vital for our health and well-being. A diet lacking in vitamins can result in serious diseases like scurvy or in malnutrition.

Yeast: yellowish, frothy substance which produces alcohol when in contact with sugar. It is used in wine-making and beer brewing and causes bread to rise.

■ Have you heard these expressions?

Bread
'The bread winner':
the wage earner in a family.
'Those will sell like
hot cakes':
those will sell very fast.

Eggs
'He's a good egg':
he's all right – he's
a decent person.
'Don't teach your
grandmother to suck eggs':
don't presume to advise
someone who is more
experienced than you are.

Fruit and vegetables
'You're the apple
of his eye':
you're his favourite.
'You're full of beans':
you're in high spirits.
'She had two bites
at the cherry':
she had a second
chance at it.
'That's a hot potato':
that's a touchy subject.
'You know your onions':
you know your job,
or your subject, well.

Cheese
'I'm feeling cheesed off':
I'm feeling fed up
'She's a big cheese':
she's very important.
'Hard cheese':
bad luck

Milk
'There's no use in crying
over spilt milk':
there's no point in
moaning about a mistake
after the damage has
been done.

Fish
'A fish out of water':
a person in an unsuitable or unaccustomed situation.
'I have other fish to fry':
I have other business to attend to.
'A red herring':
a subject introduced to divert attention. (A red herring
is literally a dried herring, with a strong smell. During a
hunt, it was sometimes drawn across a trail to put the
hounds off the scent.)

Animals
'You'll have to wait till the cows come home':
you'll have to wait for a long time.
'I could eat a horse':
I am very hungry.
'A pig in a poke':
an object bought as a bargain, but unseen
(a poke was a sort of sack.)
'You've got a bee in your bonnet':
you are obsessed with a particular idea.

'I think you're the bee's knees':
I think you're someone very special.
'Don't count your chickens before they're hatched':
don't depend too much on some uncertain future event.
'It's lovely weather for ducks':
it's very wet.
'To take the bull by the horns':
to grapple with a problem without dithering
'A bull in a china shop':
an insensitive person in a delicate situation

Salt
'I should take it with a pinch of salt':
I shouldn't believe every word of that.
'To rub salt in a wound':
to make a bad situation even worse, usually by saying
the wrong thing.

Tea
'That's not at all my cup
of tea':
that's not the sort of thing
I like.
'I wouldn't do that for all
the tea in China':
nothing would make me
do that.

General sayings
'Too many cooks spoil
the broth':
too many people trying
to do the same job get
in each other's way.
'You've bitten off more
than you can chew':
you've taken on something
that's too much for you
to cope with..
'Hunger is the best sauce':
when you are hungry,
almost any food tastes
delicious.
'To eat your heart out':
to pine away.
'To eat your words':
to take back what
you have said.
'You reap what you sow':
you get back from life
what you put into it.
'Variety is the spice of life':
doing lots of different
things makes life more
interesting.
'To have all four feet
in the trough':
to be completely involved
in eating
'To be on the breadline':
to be poor (having only
enough money to buy
food)
'To put something
on the back-burner':
to put an idea or a plan
to one side for a while and
come back to it later.
'What's cooking?':
What's going on?

A BALANCED DIET

We eat a balanced diet in order to give our body everything it needs.

What we need

Proteins Our muscles, skin and hair are made of proteins. Our cells need proteins to grow and to repair themselves.

Carbohydrates provide us with energy, which is measured in kilocalories or kilojoules.

Fibre is a special type of carbohydrate which is necessary for healthy digestion.

Fats and oils contain vitamins, allow our body to store energy, make cell walls and help our nervous and hormone systems to work well. They also protect our organs.

Minerals are vital for healthy bones, teeth and blood. They help us to contract and relax our muscles. They help to regulate the balance of fluid in our body.

Vitamins, like minerals, are essential for growth, and wellbeing.

What is a balanced diet?
It is a range of healthy foods eaten in the right variety and in sensible quantities.

The foods we eat must provide our body with: proteins, carbohydrates and fibre, fats and oils, minerals and vitamins. These are the nutrients essential to the body.

All these nutrients, in their different ways, give us energy and help to build, maintain and protect our body, so that we feel well as we work and play, run and rest.

We are what we eat!
If we eat a good balanced diet, we give our body every chance to keep fit and healthy.
Even simple meals like the contents of your lunch-box can be made to be varied and wholesome.

To find out more about diet and health, you can write to:
The Health Education Authority
Hamilton House
Mabledon Place
London WC1

Where we find what we need

Beans: protein, carbohydrate, fibre, minerals, vitamins

Bread: carbohydrate, fibre, minerals, vitamins

Eggs: protein, minerals, vitamins

Fish: protein, oils, minerals, vitamins

Fresh vegetables and fruit: fibre, minerals, vitamins

Margarines and oils: oil, vitamins

Meat: protein, fat, minerals, vitamins

Milk, butter, yoghurt, cheese: protein, fats, minerals, vitamins

Muesli and wholegrain cereals: carbohydrate, fibre, minerals, vitamins

Nuts and seeds: protein, oils, minerals, vitamins

Pasta: carbohydrate

Potatoes: carbohydrate, minerals, vitamins

Rice: carbohydrate, protein, minerals, vitamins

Lovely food for a party, but not for your everyday balanced diet!